WEATHER
Lightning

by Ann Herriges

Note to Librarians, Teachers, and Parents:

Blastoff! Readers are carefully developed by literacy experts and combine standards-based content with developmentally appropriate text.

Level 1 provides the most support through repetition of high-frequency words, light text, predictable sentence patterns, and strong visual support.

Level 2 offers early readers a bit more challenge through varied simple sentences, increased text load, and less repetition of high-frequency words.

Level 3 advances early-fluent readers toward fluency through increased text and concept load, less reliance on visuals, longer sentences, and more literary language.

Whichever book is right for your reader, Blastoff! Readers are the perfect books to build confidence and encourage a love of reading that will last a lifetime!

This edition first published in 2007 by Bellwether Media.

No part of this publication may be reproduced in whole or in part without written permission of the publisher. For information regarding permission, write to Bellwether Media Inc., Attention: Permissions Department, Post Office Box 1C, Minnetonka, MN 55345-9998.

Library of Congress Cataloging-in-Publication Data
Herriges, Ann.
 Lightning / by Ann Herriges.
   p. cm. — (Blastoff! readers) (Weather)
Summary: "Simple text and supportive images introduce beginning readers to the characteristics of lightning. Intended for students in kindergarten through third grade."
 Includes bibliographical references and index.
 ISBN-10: 1-60014-025-4 (hardcover : alk. paper)
 ISBN-13: 978-1-60014-025-9 (hardcover : alk. paper)
 1. Lightning—Juvenile literature. 2. Weather—Juvenile literature. I. Title. II. Series.

 QC966.5.H47 2007
 551.56'32—dc22   2006000616

Table of Contents

Lightning is a flash of light from a **thunderstorm**.

Lightning makes a crooked line
across the sky. Or it lights up
the **clouds**.

Storm clouds are made of tiny water drops and ice **crystals**. The air inside a storm cloud rushes up and down. The ice crystals move fast and bump into each other.

This movement makes **electricity**. The electricity grows stronger. Then lightning flashes. *Zap!* Clouds make lightning to get rid of electricity.

Lightning **bolts** make paths through the air. Most lightning bolts are about as thick as your big toe.

Lightning is fast. It can travel up to 60,000 miles (96,560 kilometers) per second.

Most lightning happens inside a storm cloud. The cloud can look like it is glowing. Or it can look like bolts are crawling around the cloud.

Sometimes lightning jumps from one cloud to another.

Lightning zigzags down from a storm cloud too.

Sometimes the lightning breaks into many bolts.

A lightning bolt can hit the ground.
This happens because the ground
under the cloud holds electricity.

A bolt travels partway from the cloud to the ground. It causes another bolt to shoot up from the ground. The two bolts meet. Lightning flashes up to the cloud.

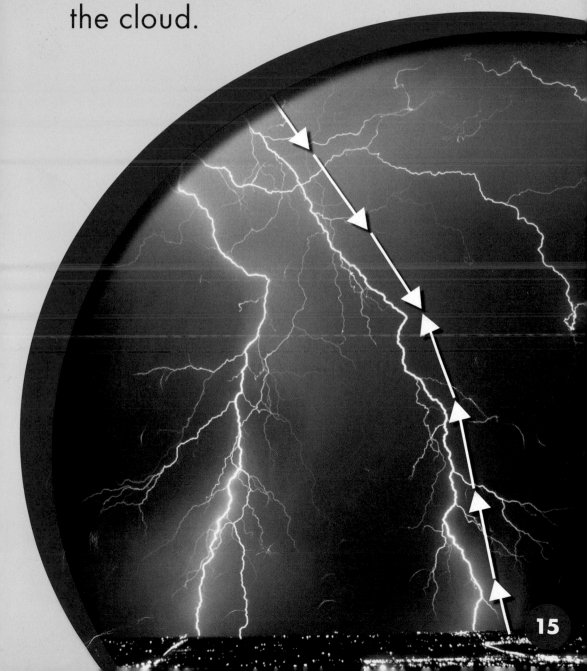

Every lightning flash makes thunder.
Lightning is very hot. It heats the air.

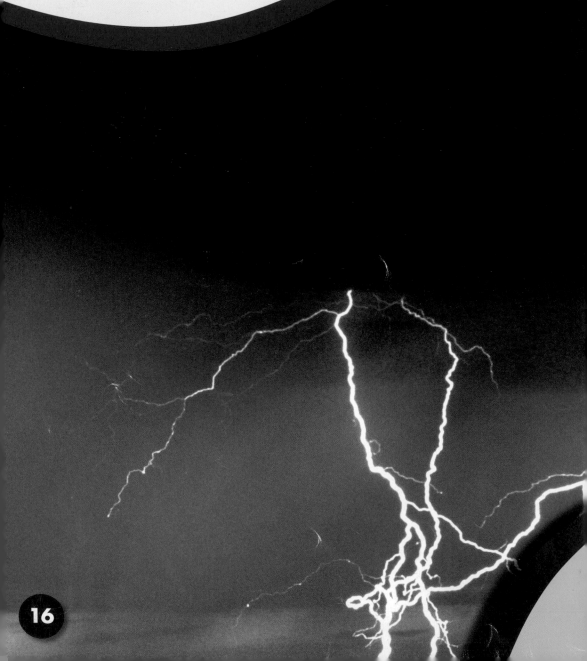

The heated air **explodes**. *Crash!*
This is thunder. The sound booms
and rumbles through the air.

17

Lightning and thunder happen at the same time. But light travels faster than sound.

You will see the flash of lightning
first. Then you will hear the thunder.

Lightning is dangerous. Go indoors when a thunderstorm is coming.

Stay low to the ground if you are outside. Lightning usually strikes the tallest objects.

Glossary

bolt—a flash of lightning

cloud—tiny drops of water or crystals of ice that float together in the air

crystal—a solid that has a pattern of many flat sides; an ice crystal is water frozen into a six-sided solid.

electricity—energy that powers lights and machines

explode—to blow apart with great force and a loud bang

thunderstorm—strong weather with high winds, lightning, and rain

To Learn More

AT THE LIBRARY

Branley, Franklyn M. *Flash, Crash, Rumble, and Roll.* New York: HarperCollins, 1999.

Bryan, Ashley. *The Story of Lightning and Thunder.* New York: Atheneum, 1993.

Dussling, Jennifer. *Lightning: It's Electrifying.* New York: Grosset & Dunlap, 2002.

Gibbons, Gail. *Weather Words and What They Mean.* New York: Holiday House, 1990.

Schanzer, Rosalyn. *How Ben Franklin Stole the Lightning.* New York: HarperCollins, 2003.

ON THE WEB

Learning more about the weather is as easy as 1, 2, 3.

1. Go to www.factsurfer.com

2. Enter "weather" into search box.

3. Click the "Surf" button and you will see a list of related web sites.

With factsurfer.com, finding more information is just a click away.

Index

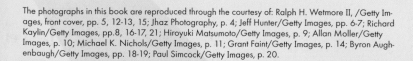